Kylee on the Go!
BELiZE

Written by
Akeem Genus & Kaya Hamer-Small

Published by Motivated and Global Media

ISBN: 978-1-7377971-0-4

The moral right of the author has been asserted.

Book Design by Uzuri Designs
www.uzuridesignsbooks.com
bookdesigner@uzuridesignsbooks.com

Dedicated to our daughter.
We hope to show you the world so that
you see there's no limit to who you can be.
May you stay curious and embrace
the adventure of life.

After a long school term,
Kylee is excited for her trip to Belize.
In school, she's been reading
and learning about Central America.

Kylee and her family arrive in Belize,
The short flight from Florida makes it feel near.
Upon landing, the humid air
makes Kylee happy to have curly hair.

On the first day in Belize, Kylee
travels to the cayes.
The water is so clear there's
nothing you can't see.

She has such a fun day
swimming and snorkeling,
she smiles with glee.

The next day Kylee and her family drive to Crooked Tree.

She is in awe of all the colorful birds flying free.

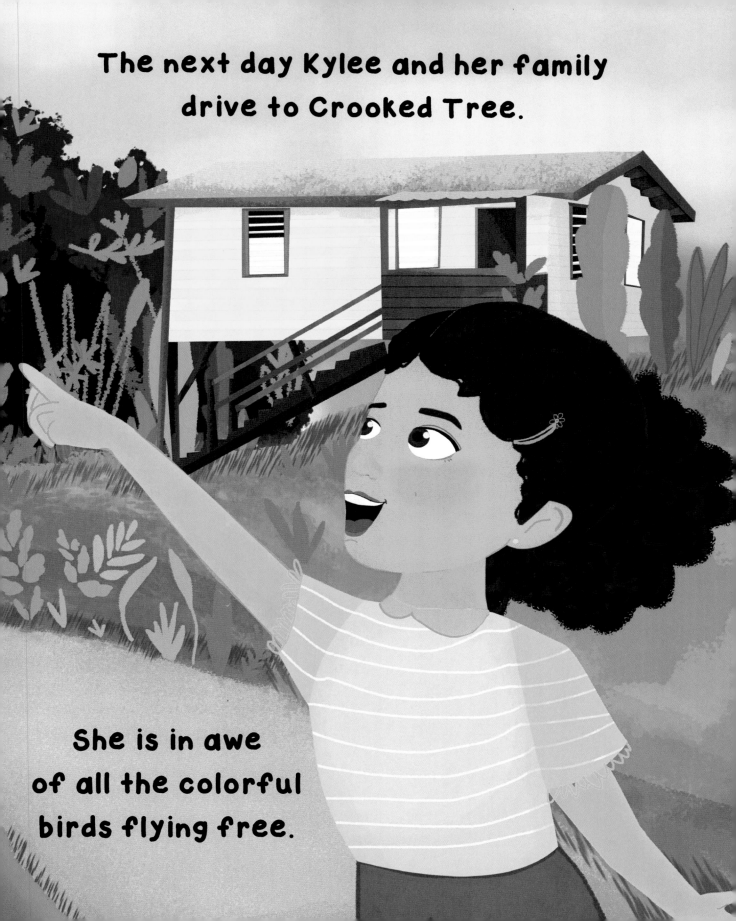

Up next, Kylee and her family
head to Cayo.
Kylee visits a Maya temple.
The howler monkeys make her tremble.

The day is hot, which calls for
a stop to swim at Big Rock Falls.

Kylee looks up and
feels so small.

After her swim, Kylee is hungry and so she stops for a local dish.

She rubs her belly happy that she ate the panades with fish!

After a good
night's sleep,
Kylee and her family
hit the road early.
They drive along
Mountain Pine Ridge.

The air is so cool it
feels like a fridge.

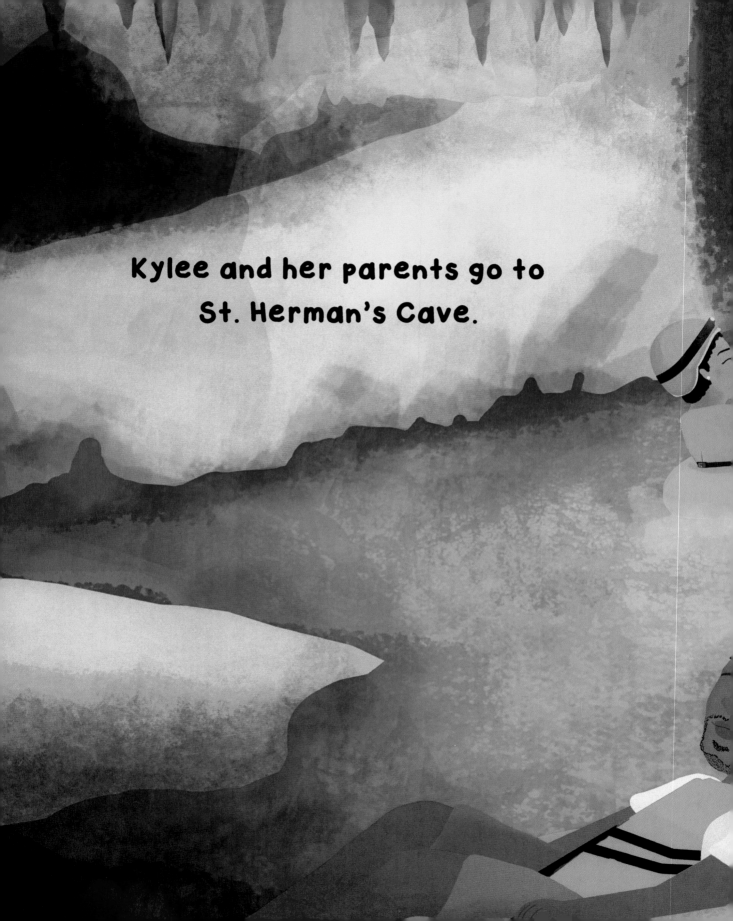

Kylee and her parents go to
St. Herman's Cave.

When she comes out,
she feels so brave.

Nearby, Daddy
even goes for a zip-line.
Kylee wants to go too,
but Mama says
maybe next time.

As the trip is coming
to an end,
Kylee stops
in Hopkins.

The Garifuna are singing,
and drums are knocking.

Kylee has a great trip
to Belize.
It is somewhere that
you must see to believe!

Crooked
Tree

Belize
City

BELMOPAN
★

Mountain
Pine Ridge

Hopkins

Five fun facts about Belize

1. Belize is the only English speaking country in Central America.

2. The Belize Barrier Reef System is the second largest in the world.

3. Belize, along with neighboring countries, was a part of the Mayan civilization.

4. Belize is home to many diverse cultures, speaking many different languages.

5. The Belizean flag is unique! It has the most colors used of any national flag.

"Travel is the best teacher in life!"
- Not a cliché, but rather the words that Akeem and Kaya live by.

Akeem and Kaya have been traveling together for over a decade. As they experienced the different countries and cultures across the world, the curiosity that is often lost in adulthood has always traveled with them no matter where they are in the world. It is that same spirit that they hope to capture through Kylee's adventures. Children's imaginations, dreams, and ultimately their mindsets are shaped by what they see around them. Through Kylee's story and how it is visually illustrated, the authors hope to spark children's imaginations and ignite their curiosity about people, places, and the cultures of the world."

Made in the USA
Las Vegas, NV
12 December 2022

61943116R10021